DIGITAL CAREER BUILDING™

CAREER BUILDING THROUGH

USING DIGITAL DESIGN TOOLS

EDWARD WILLETT

ROSEN
PUBLISHING®

New York

Published in 2014 by The Rosen Publishing Group, Inc.
29 East 21st Street, New York, NY 10010

First Edition

Library of Congress Cataloging-in-Publication Data

Willett, Edward, 1959–
Career building through using digital design tools/Edward Willett.
    pages cm.—(Digital career building)
Includes bibliographical references and index.
ISBN 978-1-4777-1723-3 (library binding)—
ISBN 978-1-4777-1739-4 (pbk.)—
ISBN 978-1-4777-1740-0 (6-pack)
1. Computer-aided design—Vocational guidance—Juvenile literature.
I. Title.
TA345.W54 2014
620'.00420285—dc23

                                                          2013017220

Manufactured in the United States of America

CPSIA Compliance Information: Batch #W14YA: For further information, contact Rosen Publishing, New York, New York, at 1-800-237-9932.

CONTENTS

CHAPTER ONE

DESIGNING THE LOOK OF THE WORLD

The world is full of visual imagery. Wherever you are right now, take a look around. From the covers of books to the ads in magazines, from the graphics in your favorite computer game to the special effects in your favorite television show, from the Web sites you visit every day to the billboards you pass on the way to school, you are surrounded by graphics. All of those graphics were designed by someone just like you—someone who started with a mental image and made that image a reality.

Once upon a time, the tools of the graphic designer were physical: pen and ink, paint and paper, glue and scissors. Today, most images you see were designed using powerful computer hardware and software. These tools enable designers to achieve effects that once would have been almost impossible.

Design has become *digital* design, and the field of digital design offers immense opportunities for creative young people. It is a field in which imagination, skill, and hard work can pay off in a long, satisfying career.

Before Design Was Digital

Although American book designer William Addison Dwiggins coined the term "graphic design" in 1922, the activity is almost as old as humanity itself. After all, ancient cave paintings are a form of graphic design: they involve the use of imagery to communicate ideas. So do stained-glass windows in cathedrals, medieval illuminated manuscripts, nineteenth-century newspaper editorial cartoons, and many other creations.

Modern graphic design really took off in the twentieth century with the rise of consumerism, especially after the Second World War as the American economy boomed. More choices for consumers meant there was a greater need for eye-catching advertising and packaging. In newspapers and magazines, on billboards, and increasingly on television, graphic designers competed for the attention of viewers.

For a more detailed look at the history of design, check out *A Short Introduction to Graphic Design History* at http://www.designhistory.org, created by designer Nancy Stock-Allen, professor at the Moore College of Art & Design in Philadelphia, Pennsylvania, for more than two decades.

There are three main elements of graphic design. First, there is artwork. Designers may create images—photographs, paintings, drawings, computer-generated graphics—especially for a design, or they may repurpose preexisting images.

Next comes typography. Although some graphic design is purely visual, most includes some text. Creating the look of that text is an important element of the overall design. The process includes choosing fonts and colors, positioning the text, adjusting its size, choosing where to break lines of text, and much more. Text isn't just words to read; it is a graphic element in its own right.

Finally, there is page layout, or how the typography and artwork are arranged on the page to best capture attention and communicate ideas.

The tools used to create graphic design may have changed over the years, but the three basic elements—artwork, typography, and page layout—have not.

Graphic designers have focused on the interplay of these three elements for decades. But the tools they use to produce these elements changed greatly beginning in the 1980s. Since then, this evolution has only accelerated. The agent of change was the personal computer.

How Graphic Design Went Digital

Before the late 1970s, personal computers were not available. Even as they first began to appear, they had little impact on the design world. They were expensive, not very powerful, had little software available, and weren't particularly easy to use.

Apple Computer, founded in 1976 by Steve Jobs and Steve Wozniak, set out to change that. The company wanted to create computers that the average person could use. People took to them in droves: by 1982, Apple had become the first personal computer company to exceed $1 billion in annual sales.

In 1983, Apple's Lisa computer introduced the notions of windows, menus, icons, and a mouse. Then, in 1984, the first Macintosh appeared. Two years later, Apple introduced the more powerful Mac Plus. Along with other developments, Apple's machines gave graphic designers a whole new way to create—and opened up graphic design to many more people.

IBM came out with its own, more powerful personal computer in 1981. However, the ease of use and graphical user interface (GUI) of Macintosh computers made them the go-to machines for designers. To this day, even though Windows-based computers also offer a graphical user interface, Apple is still extremely popular among designers.

The Birth of Desktop Publishing

One of the key developments that turned graphic design digital was the invention of desktop publishing. It gave individuals the ability to do things that previously required entire graphic design and printing shops. Three companies produced the key technologies: Apple, Adobe, and Aldus (later bought by Adobe). To a large degree, Apple hardware and Adobe software still drive digital design today.

The Apple Macintosh computer provided an easy-to-use interface that allowed people without specialized computer skills to simulate their normal working environment: a workspace on a desktop. PageMaker, released in 1985 by Aldus, was the first desktop publishing software. It allowed designers to lay out pages in a mode known as WYSIWYG ("What You See Is What You Get"), instead of having to use complex code commands.

 The release of the first Apple Macintosh computer in 1984 was one of the key elements in the development of desktop publishing—and modern digital design.

The computer language PostScript allowed graphic designers' projects—both text and artwork—to be accurately reproduced by any PostScript-enabled device. Apple's LaserWriter printer, released the same year as PageMaker, was the first such printer available to the mass market.

The desktop publishing revolution happened with astonishing speed. The age of digital design had begun.

A CLOSER LOOK Interested in the history of computers? The Computer History Museum in Mountain View, California, has a Web site full of virtual exhibits on various computer history topics. Visit http://www.computerhistory.org.

Today, Adobe Systems Incorporated makes the bulk of industry-standard software programs for designers. These include Photoshop for photo editing, Illustrator for drawing, InDesign for page design, and Dreamweaver for Web site design.

This brings up another way in which the digital revolution changed graphic design. In 1993, Tim Berners-Lee created a new way for computers to communicate with each other over the existing Internet: the World Wide Web. Within an astonishingly short time, the Web became an integral part of society. Now there are billions of Web pages, and these Web pages need designers. Just as in the bookstore or the grocery store, the competition for eyeballs is fierce. Web page design, though it includes the time-honored triumvirate

Web page design combines not only the classic elements of graphic design but also user interface design, coding, animation, and more.

of artwork, typography, and page layout, involves user interface design (determining how people interact with the Web site), coding, animation, and more.

Web design is not the only way in which digital tools have revolutionized design. Digital tools are now used for all kinds of design, from the design of automobiles to the design of buildings. In the not too distant future, the advent of low-cost 3-D printing will allow designs created on a computer to be turned into real-world objects, from toys to tools.

What's in It for Me?

Digital design is a wide-open field. The hardware and software required are inexpensive and are getting cheaper all the time. Age is no barrier: many well-known designers got their start as teenagers.

Because digital design is everywhere, it offers end-less ways to get started. Maybe you can't design a major corporation's Web site yet, but you can design one for a local sports team. You might not be ready to manipulate images of high-fashion models for *Vogue*, but you can offer to retouch your neighbors' family photos. Take every informal opportunity that presents itself to learn how to use digital design tools, take formal training when you can, and above all, practice, practice, practice.

The number-one tool for any designer is a creative mind. Cultivate that, and everything else you will read about here will follow. Then you, too, can have a career as a digital designer.

CHAPTER TWO

GOOD DESIGN AND GOOD DESIGNERS

If you want to be a designer, you need to study the design that's all around you. Pay attention to what works and what doesn't work. This will help you develop your own sense of design. Design is everywhere. Here are just a few places to look for it.

Corporate Identity

We live in an era of logos: they seem to be on everything, from clothing to cars. Typically, the logo is just the most visible element of a graphic identity for a company. This identity includes everything from stationery and signage to advertising and annual reports.

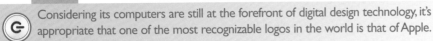

Considering its computers are still at the forefront of digital design technology, it's appropriate that one of the most recognizable logos in the world is that of Apple.

The designers who create corporate identities are trying to boil down complex concepts into distinctive visual elements that communicate what the company does, how it is positioned in the market, and even its attitude—from staid and professional to hip and loose.

Packaging

Closely allied with corporate identity and branding is packaging design. The special challenge of designing packaging is that the design is linked to a three-dimensional object. Text and images may have to wrap around corners or weave around plastic bubbles.

In addition, packaging has to capture hurried people's attention in the visually cluttered environment of a store. It has to work not only from far away (to attract the shopper's eye) but also up close, as the shopper examines the product to see if he or she wants to buy it. It combines branding, advertising, and information design.

Packaging designers often work closely with the designers of brand identity and the designers of the structure of the package in a highly collaborative process.

Signs

"Signs, signs, everywhere a sign," sang the Five Man Electrical Band in 1971. Back then, signs were often hand painted. Now they are designed and printed using computers. But they are still everywhere.

Sign designers have to be concerned not just with creating a beautiful sign; they also have to be aware of the sign's purpose and location. A sign that will be read in the brief moment of attention it can capture from a passing motorist can't be too cluttered. A sign directing people to the nearest restroom better not be so clever that they can't tell whether it is pointing to the men's or women's room, or it invites disaster.

Signs must take into account a lot of things outside the designer's control, such as lighting or the color of nearby walls. Sign designers, therefore, often work with architects and interior designers.

Editorial Design

Editorial design is the design of magazines, newspapers, and books. In magazine design, more elements of digital design come together than in almost any other kind of design. A strong sense of typography and composition

Many designers are employed in magazine and book design. Here, a designer works on the magazine and Web layouts for *The Knot*, a print and online source for wedding planning information in New York City.

is essential, as images, illustrations, headlines, and more come together in a unique combination created with equal parts technical skill and artistic flair.

Editorial design requires constant reinvention. There is always another issue or book title to design. Although each publication has its own templates and design rules, the challenge is to create something new and fresh within those rules.

Web Design

Early Web sites were little more than pages of text with hyperlinks to other pages of text. But with growing computing power and network speed, Web sites have come to include everything from high-end graphics to full-motion video, sound, complex user interactions, and data mining. New design challenges have arisen as more and more people access Web sites through mobile devices, whose smaller screens necessitate changes in design.

Web sites for businesses and organizations may be called upon to perform a multitude of tasks, often simultaneously. Skilled designers who can create sites that both look beautiful and work well are always in demand.

Game and Motion Picture Design

Video games are now a multibillion-dollar industry. Developing games requires the talent of digital designers to create the interface, characters, backgrounds, and more. Video game designers have to be talented 2-D and 3-D artists, as well as knowledgeable about computer hardware and software. They must be enormously creative, able to work fast, and have strong problem-solving skills. (Naturally, they also need to appreciate and play video games. Know anybody like that?)

Television shows, movies, and Webcasts need digital designers, especially with the growth of entertainment heavy in special effects. Like video games, some require the creation of entire fictional worlds from scratch. The work may take place out of the limelight, but without the designers, most television programs and movies would never make it to the screen.

Product Design

One reason Apple enjoys the enviable place it does in the business world is outstanding design. Apple devices have a unique look that sets them apart. Good product design involves working in three dimensions rather than two,

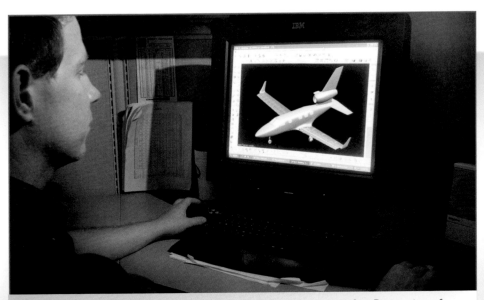

An engineer with Piper Aircraft, Inc., designs wing parts for Piper aircraft at the company's plant in Vero Beach, Florida. Digital design extends into the three-dimensional as well as the two-dimensional world.

and must take into account functionality as well as appearance. (It is easy to design a fictional automobile that looks amazing; it is a lot harder to keep those creative features while also dealing with safety requirements, engines, tires, etc.) Even more than other forms of design, product design is a highly collaborative effort.

Those are just a few examples of places to look for good design—and the kinds of projects you, as a digital designer, might be working on someday. But what about the designers themselves? Who are they, and how did they get started? There are thousands of great designers. Here are four: two men and two women.

Shane Mielke

A designer and creative director at 2Advanced Studios in Aliso Viejo, Californa, Mielke specializes in design, development, motion, and photography. He has worked for many major brands, including Activision, Ford, LucasArts, TaylorMade Golf, Warner Brothers, and more.

Mielke became interested in design thanks to a college friend who experimented a lot with print, 3-D, and video design. In an interview with the online magazine .net, Mielke said, "I was always looking over his shoulder when he was designing, and the things he created captivated me. After I graduated, a close friend of mine was working for a small Web company and I started learning things from him. The rest is history."

He said playing football also contributed to his success. "I'd say that the hard work, teamwork, problem solving, and pain tolerance I learned in American football has directly translated to how I handle work. I once stayed up fifty-six hours to meet a deadline, but it felt easy compared to what I went through on the football field."

Mielke's advice: "Surround yourself with people who have the skills you want and are the type of people you want to be."

Rachel Shillcock

Rachel Shillcock is a Web designer, front-end developer, graphic designer, logo author, and award-winning photographer from the north of England. She writes for industry-leading magazines and online publications and is a frequent conference speaker.

As a child, Shillcock first wanted to be a veterinarian. Then she got hold of her father's old business computer and started browsing the Web. She didn't know anything about coding, but she started doing design work just for fun, experimenting with a copy of Photoshop that she bought on eBay. She told the networking organization Second Wednesday, "I started playing around with blending photographs and that sort of evolved into thinking, 'Well, actually now I can do that. I want to know more.' I started to figure out what sites were, how they were made, and following all sorts of tutorials."

She struggled in college, but during that time joined Twitter, which she credits with helping her make the connections that helped her build her career. "Your portfolio is the most important asset you'll have," she wrote in a story for *.net* magazine. "Find as much work experience as you can. Do placements at as many agencies as possible, work for charities and—although it can

Design for the Future: 3-D Printing

Most digital design is still intended for the 2-D world of page or screen. But we are at the threshold of an era when you will be able to design 3-D objects on the computer and print them out much like you print 2-D designs today.

Imagine a future in which you buy, say, a pair of new sunglasses online, download the design from the Internet, and then print the item yourself using a device in your own home or in a corner 3-D print shop. The current economic model of mass production, stockpiling, and distribution of physical objects could someday seem a quaint relic of the past.

3-D printing works by building up objects in a series of very thin layers. There are various technologies. Some make use of photopolymer, a liquid that hardens when exposed to ultraviolet light. In one method, a laser traces the object layer by layer, printing an entire cross-section with a projector. In another, an inkjet-style print head jets out the liquid for each layer; then a UV light solidifies it before the next layer is printed. Some printers extrude a semiliquid material such as a hot thermoplastic. However, the material doesn't have to be plastic—there are cheese printers, chocolate printers, and even concrete printers.

Another type of 3-D printing uses a powdered building material, which is stuck together with a binding agent extruded from a print head or using heat. This method allows for 3-D printing using numerous materials, including wax, polystyrene, nylon, glass, stainless steel, titanium, and various alloys.

Commercial/industrial 3-D printers still cost tens of thousands of dollars. However, freelance designers can already obtain quality 3-D printouts by using an online service such as

Shapeways, iMaterialize, or Sculpteo. Also, personal 3-D printers are rapidly becoming available and affordable.

Although most 3-D printers are being used for rapid product prototyping or to create molds for finished products, some finished products—ranging from lighting to jewelry—are already emerging from printers. In the future, spare parts, entire buildings, aircraft, automobiles, and even replacement organs may be 3-D printed. The possibilities are amazing, and the opportunities for talented designers are endless.

 Three-dimensional printing offers exciting opportunities for digital designers. The printers are becoming more and more widespread and accessible—like this one a teen examines at the Westport Public Library in Connecticut.

be difficult—offer to do some unpaid projects for exposure." Equally important, she said, is creating a strong online presence. "What good is a project if nobody knows about it?" she wrote.

Shillcock's most important advice? "Love what you do. Pour everything you are into it, and eventually you'll be great."

 RepRap is an online community aimed at making self-replicating machines— 3-D printers that can print their own components—and making them freely available for the benefit of everyone. Everything is open source. Read all about at it at http://www.reprap.org.

Tyler Galpin

Tyler Galpin is a Web, user interface (UI), logo, typeface, and T-shirt designer from Toronto, Canada, and the founder of his own business, Galpin Industries, also based in Toronto.

Galpin began designing for fun when he was fourteen. By the time he was nineteen, he was designing professionally. He told blogger and fellow designer Yassine Bentaieb, "At our school we were required to have a laptop, and as a kid you really want yours to stand out. We would go on sites like Deviantart and try and find awesome wallpapers to style our computers. I wanted to learn and make some wallpapers for myself— that's how I really got started with design."

He made his first Web site for a media arts class in eleventh grade. His first serious work came in college, when he did some freelance work for people he knew. He also did free work for various conferences and charities to get his name noticed and to hone his skills.

According to Galpin, "There is no better time to be a designer than right now. As long as you have a design eye...and you work really hard, that's pretty much the only formula you need to be successful."

Want to read about more great designers? The Web site Creativeoverflow has a list of twenty-four graphic designers you can follow on Google+ at http://creativeoverflow .net/24-graphic-designers-to-follow-on-google.

Sarah Parmenter

A multidisciplinary designer from Essex, England, Sarah Parmenter is the owner of the design studio You Know Who, also based in Essex. Her impressive list of clients includes BlackBerry, News International, STV, and the National Breast Cancer Foundation. Parmenter, who specializes in interface design for Apple's iOS, was voted *.net* magazine's Designer of the Year in 2011.

She started her business at age nineteen. On her Web site, http://www.sazzy.co.uk, she said, "It's only now, looking at other nineteen-year-olds, do I realize how young I was to be delving into the business world and living without a lot of money." Still, she is glad she risked it when she did. She explained, "When you get older and you have the pressure of mortgages, bills, and such like, it's not so easy to throw caution to the wind in the same way."

Parmenter studied fine art at a school that didn't have any facilities for doing graphic design on a computer. She learned on her own, using a computer to manipulate imagery that she first created at school with pencil and paper. She still starts her projects on paper and moves them to the Mac.

Her best advice for newbie designers is: "Take baby steps, and never stop learning. If you learn a little bit each day, you'll build up to enough knowledge to start doing something great with it."

She also has advice for young women in particular. "Don't let being in a male-dominated environment make an ounce of difference to the way you do business," she said on her Web site. "It's never adversely affected me. As long as you keep your head down, work hard, and produce good work, no one can ever accuse you of not doing your best."

CHAPTER THREE
FIRST STEPS: GETTING STARTED IN DIGITAL DESIGN

As the brief biographies of the designers in the previous section prove, there is no one way to break into digital design. Still, there are some general principles to keep in mind that may help you turn your fledgling skills and interest into a rewarding—and hopefully, profitable—career.

Start Small

As the Chinese proverb famously has it, "A journey of a thousand miles begins with a single step." Start taking on projects right now from people in your circle of acquaintances. Is your friend starting a band? Offer to set up the group's Web site. Does your brother have a small business? Help him come up with a company identity.

Do you or members of your family belong to any local organizations? It could be a community theater group, a house of worship, or a local charity. Even the smallest organization needs to communicate with its members and the outside world. These days, that probably means maintaining a Web site and a print or digital newsletter. It might also include a presence on social media. Find out what's needed and offer to provide it.

You may or may not get paid, but don't worry about it. This kind of work isn't about earning money—it's about getting experience. Your "client" may simply be the band of your guitar-playing buddy who thinks he's the new Jimi Hendrix. However, the process of figuring

When you're starting out, any design experience you can get is valuable—even if it's low-paying or volunteer work.

out the best way to communicate what the band and its music are all about is the same as the process you'd follow when designing for, say, Atlantic Records. And working with the board of directors of a community theater company is no different from working with the board of directors of a major entertainment consortium. You're still trying to come up with a design that will communicate information to audiences in a way that makes them happy.

The best way to improve as a designer is to do more designing. Working for free on small projects lets you build your skills—and learn from your mistakes— in an environment where the stakes are relatively low. As you start making fewer mistakes and achieving more successes, you will build confidence and something even more important: a portfolio.

Not sure what your online portfolio should look like? *Smashing Magazine* has compiled a selection of fifty beautiful and creative portfolio designs at http://www .smashingmagazine.com/2008/11/26/50-beautiful-and -creative-portfolio-designs.

Once upon a time, a portfolio was a big folder or binder into which designers would put samples of their best work. These days, most portfolios are online. Visit any designer's Web site, and you will find examples of his or her work. Once you have a few samples of work that you are really proud of, you can put them in your own online portfolio.

Essential Software: Adobe Creative Cloud

What software do you need to be a digital designer? The industry standard has long been Adobe's Creative Suite. In 2013, Adobe announced that future versions of the software products would be available only on a subscription basis. For a monthly fee, subscribers to Adobe Creative Cloud can get access to the latest versions of these powerful, professional tools. Students can subscribe at a lower rate for their first year. The tools include:

- Photoshop, the standard in photo-correction and manipulation software
- Illustrator, the standard in 64-bit vector drawing
- InDesign, the standard in page design software, whether for professional printing or desktop publishing
- Dreamweaver, for creating Web sites and apps for smartphones, tablets, and desktop computers
- Flash Professional, for designing immersive interactive experiences and games that can be used on desktops, smartphones, tablets, and televisions
- Premiere, top-notch video editing software
- After Effects, for creating visual effects and motion graphics
- Audition, a professional program for audio editing and mixing

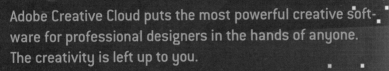

Adobe Creative Cloud puts the most powerful creative software for professional designers in the hands of anyone. The creativity is left up to you.

CORE CREATIVE TOOLS   INTERACTIVE MEDIA TOOLS   PUBLISHING

David Wadhwani, an executive at Adobe Systems, Inc., speaks at the launch of Adobe Creative Cloud and Creative Suite 6 in San Francisco, California, in April 2012. Designers can now obtain Adobe's industry-standard design tools via subscription.

Of course, one of the design projects you should undertake very early on is setting up your own Web site. This should be a place where people looking for designers can go to find out more about you and the skills you can bring to the table. Keep examples of your very best work online where prospective clients can find it. You never know who might be looking.

Take It Up a Notch

With a few projects under your belt, your skills improving, and your portfolio online, you can start to branch out from friends and family into the wider community. Digital design is everywhere, and that means design opportunities are everywhere.

Study the Web sites and publications of local businesses and organizations. Do you see things that need improving? Do you think you could offer a solution? Contact organizations and make them aware of your services. They may already have a relationship with a designer, but maybe they hire freelancers and would be open to hiring a different one the next time. At the very least, you are getting your name out there and making those all-important contacts.

Of course, you should also look for businesses and organizations that *don't* have an online presence or whose newsletter is little more than a sheet of text. They might be even more open to an offer to design something for them for a reasonable fee.

Eventually, you will get a phone call or e-mail asking you to take on your first freelance job. And then? First and foremost, do good work. You have to work hard, do what you promised, meet your deadline, and be easy to work with. Be willing to compromise to satisfy your clients. The purpose of your design is to communicate your clients' message the way *they* want it communicated. You need to get your ego out of the way and let that happen. You don't want to get a reputation for being difficult to work with or for doing shoddy work because the word will get out to other people who are prospective customers. If your clients are happy, you can ask them to recommend you to other potential clients. If your clients aren't happy, you don't want them to talk to other prospective clients—but they will anyway.

With that first successful project under your belt, you can add it to your portfolio—and look for the next job.

Entry Points

Besides Web sites and newsletters, here are other possible entry points for a fledgling designer:

- **Brochures.** Businesses use them; so do tourist attractions. Often they aren't well designed. Offer to change that.

- **PowerPoint presentations.** Many businesses and individuals create these for use at conferences, trade shows, and the like—and many of them are pretty awful. Can you do better? Offer your services.

- **T-shirts.** Everyone from theater groups to sports teams buys customized T-shirts. You can create T-shirt designs and market them online through one of many sites that offer that service.

- **E-book covers.** Sure, major publishers employ well-established designers. But more and more writers are publishing their own books online, and they need designers, too, especially for covers. Book cover design is an art in its own right. If you study what works and you have the knack for it, it could be a profitable undertaking.

- **Business cards.** They're ubiquitous and they're often boring, but they don't have to be. They can also become a showcase for your design skills that the client hands out for you, everywhere he or she goes.

Ask if you can put a small line with your Web site on the back of the brochures, business cards, or other items you design, and they become both a way for the client to promote his or her business and a way for you to promote yours.

 Think you've got what it takes to design T-shirts that other people will want to buy? Check out Design by Humans (http://www.designbyhumans.com) and give it your best shot.

Build Mad Skillz

Of course, what will ultimately make or break your design career is your ability to do good work. That means constantly striving to do *better* work. Hone your skills every way you can. There are online tutorials, books, YouTube videos, and more offering tips on design and getting the most out of the standard design software.

Digital design tools keep changing, so never stop learning how to use the latest technology, from tablet computers to photo-editing software like this.

Every time you undertake a project, strive to make it the very best project that you've ever done. If you are not growing as a designer, you are stagnating—and falling behind all the other designers who *are* striving to do something better every time.

As your skills grow, the range of projects you can tackle will grow as well, and the range of clients you can contact for future work will expand. You will have moved several more important steps along that journey of a thousand miles to becoming a top-notch digital designer.

CHAPTER FOUR

TIME TO GET FORMAL: FORMALLY EDUCATED, THAT IS

It is entirely possible to launch a career as a designer without formal education. But there are a lot of good reasons to get formal schooling. In 2013, Parsons the New School for Design in New York City held a formal debate on the resolution "Formal design education is necessary for practicing designers." A team made up of Alice Twemlow, an educator at the School of Visual Arts in New York; Matteo Bologna, founding partner of Mucca Design, also in New York; and Abbot Miller, partner at Pentagram, headquartered in New York, set forth the arguments in favor of formal design education.

Value of a Formal Education

The debate team at Parsons compared self-education to a meal with a few inconsistent courses, in contrast to formal education, a full meal with an appropriate nutritional balance. They noted that formal education provides opportunities for classroom critiques of student work, allowing people to identify their weaknesses in an organized, productive setting. They pointed out that the guidance of experienced teachers and fellow students helps fledgling designers identify areas where they need to strengthen their knowledge and skills. In addition, they argued that formal design education enables designers to understand and embrace the rich tradition and

Formal design training offers the opportunity for fledgling designers to strengthen their skills, nurture their creativity, and try new things, all under the guidance of experienced teachers.

philosophical underpinnings of the design field. Finally, they noted that formal design education allows students an opportunity to explore the design field without commercial constraints.

 You can read more about the debate on the topic of formal education for designers at http://theindustry.cc/2013/02/20/is-formal-design-education-necessary-for-practicing-designers.

There were a couple of other arguments they didn't make but might have. One is that there are a lot of people competing for jobs with digital design agencies. Your portfolio may be impressive, but it might not be significantly more impressive than those of dozens of other young designers. If some of those other designers have a degree in design from an accredited institution, they've got a leg up on you.

A degree indicates to an agency that a candidate has had training in the many different aspects of design that he or she might encounter at work. It also shows that the candidate is committed to the craft and has already invested hundreds of hours and thousands of dollars in his or her future career. It is a signal that the designer takes design seriously.

Formal education also offers something else: connections. Your fellow students today may be your design partners in the future, or they may offer you tips or leads for work. Yes, you can craft a successful career as a self-taught designer, but there are many advantages to following the formal route.

What Will I Study?

Every design program is different, of course, but there
are some topics you can expect to study no matter which
school you attend. Everyone starts with the basics: the
concepts, vocabulary, and ideas associated with good
design. Principles of design such as balance, alignment,
repetition, consistency, and contrast, and elements of
design such as line, shape, texture, color, and movement
are the basic tools of all designers.

Basic design courses typically introduce basic
typography and layout concepts. The description of the
introductory design course at Algonquin College in
Ottawa, Ontario, Canada, sums it up like this: "Students
will see how to put design concepts into practice and
make use of fundamental principles to construct the

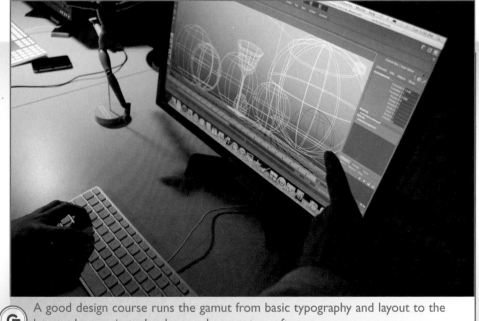

A good design course runs the gamut from basic typography and layout to the
latest advances in technology and computer software.

invisible underlying structure that is essential to effective graphic design."

The basics are expanded upon in more advanced courses. Here is Rhode Island School of Design's description of its undergraduate program in graphic design: "You'll study communications theory, design history, visual form-making, color, systems thinking, and information design along with a progression of typography courses, from the anatomy of letter forms to expressive and experimental uses of type. You'll also have the opportunity to take studios in everything from traditional book arts to interactive texts and digital media. Professors will challenge you to develop your own visual language as you create strong responses to assigned projects." The description also states that students will develop the ability to think critically and convey complex information powerfully.

An excellent design school should have a great Web site, like this one for the Rhode Island School of Design, one of the top design schools in the country.

TIME TO GET FORMAL:
FORMALLY EDUCATED, THAT IS

Where Should I Study?

Many postsecondary educational institutions, from community colleges to Ivy League universities, offer design courses. The program that suits you best may be influenced by financial concerns, living arrangements, and other factors.

Maybe you want to be able to live at home while you study to save on costs. That might limit your choices to colleges or technical schools geographically

Applying for a Digital Design Program

The specific requirements for applying to a digital design program will obviously vary from school to school, but typically you need to submit an academic transcript and, almost always, samples of your work.

As an example, Vancouver Community College in Vancouver, British Columbia, asks for ten to fifteen samples of work. One's application portfolio may include any combination of drawings, paintings, or prints; photographs, collage, or other mixed-media work; sculpture or ceramics; Web, print design, and/or communication design; sketchbooks, journals, and written work; or jewelry, architectural, and industrial design. The school says, "We value inventiveness, organization, and attention to detail. How you develop and give form to your portfolio will be important."

Creating a portfolio that will impress the admissions officers at a design school is good practice for creating a portfolio to impress prospective clients further down the road.

close to you. Maybe you need to hold down a part-time job to work your way through school, so you need to go to a city where the economy is strong enough to offer opportunities for work. You should also consider your current skill set. What are you confident you already know? What are your areas of weakness? Some schools focus more on certain aspects of design than others.

 You can extend your formal education beyond a two- or four-year undergraduate program by enrolling in a graduate program. *U.S. News & World Report* has been ranking educational programs for many years. Its list of the best U.S. graduate schools for fine arts and graphic design is at http://grad-schools.usnews.rankingsandreviews.com /best-graduate-schools/top-fine-arts-schools/graphic -design-rankings.

Many lists of recommended design schools exist online. In late 2012, for example, the Web site Business Insider conducted a survey of 633 art directors and product designers—87.8 percent of whom had themselves studied or participated in a college-level design program. The top five schools were:

• Parsons the New School for Design (http://www .newschool.edu/parsons) in New York City. In the words of one survey respondent, "The best graduate-level talent for product concept, visualization, design, and management is coming from Parsons in New York and Stanford's D School."

Parsons the New School for Design is a consistently top-rated design school in New York City. This is its David M. Schwartz Fashion Education Center.

- Carnegie Mellon University School of Design (http://www.design.cmu.edu) in Pittsburgh, Pennsylvania. One respondent called the school "a leader in the integration of arts and design with technology and user research."

- University of Cincinnati's College of Design, Architecture, Art, and Planning (http://daap .uc.edu) in Cincinnati, Ohio. The school offers a top-notch design education, plus all the amenities of a top-tier university campus.

- Massachusetts Institute of Technology Media Lab (http://www.media.mit.edu) in Cambridge, Massachusetts. Graduate John Underkoffler came up with most of the data interface ideas seen in Steven Spielberg's film *Minority Report*.

- Rhode Island School of Design (http://www.risd.edu) in Providence, Rhode Island. One of the oldest and best-known colleges of art and design in the United States, it offers rigorous bachelor's and master's degree programs in nineteen design, architecture, fine arts, and art education majors.

Formal education may not be absolutely necessary—but it may also be the difference between an average career and an outstanding one.

CHAPTER FIVE
TEN TIPS FOR DESIGNING A SUCCESSFUL DESIGN CAREER

Yͦou've got the skills. You've got the creativity. You've got the passion. You're ready to get your digital design career rolling. How can you guarantee success? Well, you can't. But here are ten tips that can maximize your chances for success.

Brand Yourself

Designers are often called upon to build a brand identity. Start with yourself: design your own logo. Make it the best logo you can create. Make it memorable, and make it consistent with your own design style and philosophy.

Design your own Web site. It should be a showcase for your skills and, again, be reflective of your approach to design. But don't get carried away: don't make it so complicated that the client is left admiring the graphics but is unable to actually find a way to contact you!

What makes a good logo? According to graphic designer Jacob Cass, an effective logo is simple, memorable, timeless, versatile, and appropriate.

Develop an Effective Online Portfolio

A good online portfolio should represent your skills across a wide range of areas, proving that you can do a lot of things and do them well. It also needs to be easily navigable. Again, don't get so carried away with clever design on your Web site that it becomes hard for visitors

A good online portfolio that showcases your best work, highlights your skills, and lists your experience—like this one for illustrator and graphic novelist Gareth Hind—is a must for any modern designer.

to find samples of your work or browse from one item to the next. Good graphic design is all about communication, and the idea you are trying to communicate is what a wonderful graphic designer you are!

Don't Neglect Print

You'll need to have a résumé, of course. It should always be complete and up to date. You'll need business cards, too. Remember, business cards are not just a way for people to retrieve your contact information but are tiny pieces of design. Your business card may not get you the job, but it may be a prospective client's first hint of your ability to do the job.

You should also have a hard copy version of your portfolio. Do you design Web sites? Create some high-quality print images of the best elements of those Web sites. With a print portfolio, you may be able to get work from the person you meet at that Wi-Fi-free lodge in the mountains, if you just "happen" to have it in the car.

Develop Good Communication Skills

Graphic design is all about communicating ideas in the most effective way possible. It's hard to convince a prospective client that you can communicate his or her message effectively if you can't communicate well yourself. When telephoning, leave a message that's pleasant, succinct, and complete; don't ramble. The same goes for e-mail. You need to strike the right balance between being friendly and too informal.

When you talk to people in person, present yourself well. Clothes matter. Your manner of speech matters. Be

The Freelance Life

Many designers have full-time jobs with agencies. Others work "freelance"—a term inspired by the mercenary knights of old, "free lances" who sold their services to whatever lord might require some muscle. The freelance life offers both pluses and minuses. On the plus side, you're the one in charge. You decide what you'll work on, when you'll work on it, and how much you'll charge for it. You can work from home, from an office, or perhaps even from the beach.

On the downside, you work alone. If you're a loner, that's fine. If you're gregarious and need people around you to keep you focused and sane, it might not be. There's no steady income: paychecks arrive at irregular intervals and sometimes don't arrive at all. The workload can be uneven, with too much work sometimes and not enough at other times. Further, a freelancer is running his or her own business and has to handle things such as advertising, taxes, and supplies that other people man-age in a graphic design agency.

All of this can create a considerable amount of stress that can affect your ability to design. The most successful free-lancers typically are those who started their careers working for others. They became knowledgeable about the design business before launching out on their own. Whether you choose to do that or be self-employed from the beginning of your career, be sure to go into it with your eyes open. It may just be your cup of tea. But don't be surprised if it's a far tougher life than you expected.

polite, professional, and friendly, but not too forward. A good personal impression will go a long way toward cementing what could be a long, profitable relationship.

Be Professional

Be prompt. Show up for meetings on time. Make phone calls when you say you'll make them. Above all, meet your deadlines. Get the work done when you say you'll get it done. Do every job to the best of your ability. "Good enough" should never be good enough.

Be courteous to the client. "The customer is always right" can be a hard adage to follow when you've poured so much of your creative juices into a project that the client second-guesses or just doesn't like. Defend your ideas, but be respectful and as flexible as you can. Even if you end up severing the relationship, do it politely. Remember, rejection of your work isn't the same as rejection of you.

Don't Be Afraid to Take on Small Jobs

There's a saying in theater: "There are no small parts, only small actors." In design, you could say there are no small jobs—only designers who don't understand the value of small projects. Some are very small indeed, such as a business card design for the owner of a local dance supply store or a brochure advertising the latest in faucets for the plumber who fixed your drains. They won't bring in much money, but they may bring in some. And when you're just starting out, some is a lot better than none. More important, you're building your skills and your reputation—and you're making connections. Word of mouth is the most powerful promotional tool of all.

Consider doing work pro bono (for free). You might design community theater programs, hospital auxiliary newsletters, or church bulletins. It's good practice, it builds goodwill, and it gets your name out into the community. And you know what? It's also just a nice thing to do.

Believe in Yourself

This is harder than it sounds when things aren't going well. You have to be confident in your own abilities while at the same time conscious of your limitations.

Don't brag, but don't be afraid to point out to clients what you've accomplished and what you're proud of. When the time comes to quote a price, don't undercut your own worth by setting your prices too low. It might get you work, but too low a price indicates that you don't think very highly of yourself—and if you don't, why should your client?

Network, Network, Network

Every connection you make with someone can lead to work.

Online networking is a powerful means of making connections. Facebook, Pinterest, Twitter, LinkedIn...all of these social media sites offer opportunities for making connections with people who may need your services or know someone who does. There are also Web sites devoted to design where you can ask questions, discuss design, and make connections with other designers.

An important part of building a successful design career is networking with other designers and keeping on top of new developments in the field. Membership in professional organizations such as AIGA can help.

There are many professional organizations for designers and artists. Joining, if you're qualified to do so, is another great way to make connections with others working in your field. Such organizations often have Web sites and publications filled with valuable information to help you build your career. The conferences and events they offer can be a great place to network and meet people in the flesh.

Networking doesn't just mean networking with other designers. Other networks—social clubs, community organizations, churches, sports teams—are valuable, too. Don't spend all your time hunched over a computer. Get involved in your community.

You may soon find there are more people than you ever imagined who could use a little assistance with digital design.

Wondering how to build your graphic design career through social media? *Speckyboy Design Magazine* has some great tips at http://www.speckyboy.com /2011/05/10/promoting-your-freelance-design -business-with-social-media.

Never Be Satisfied

Think you're pretty good? Maybe you are. But you can always—*always*—be better. The people who become great at what they do are the ones who are never satisfied, who are always trying new things, learning, growing, and improving.

Keep training. When the opportunity arises to attend a conference or a weeklong workshop, take it. Keep trying new things. You probably specialize in one or two areas of design. Don't let that stop you from taking on new challenges outside your comfort zone. You may find that you have a knack for something you never suspected.

Keep learning from others. The world is full of design. Study what impresses you, and figure out why. Study what doesn't impress you, and figure out why not.

Never Give Up

There are many talented designers out there trying to find work just like you. Some of them will get the jobs you really, really wanted. It can be hard to see work flowing to other people when you feel your own designs haven't been given a chance to shine. In any field, the biggest determinant of a successful career is often that those who succeeded never gave up.

If you have passion, talent, creativity, and perseverance, you can make a career out of your interest in digital design. Yes, it's a challenging, competitive field, but you know what? That just makes it all the more exciting.

GLOSSARY

advent The arrival of a notable thing, person, or event.

fine art Visual art that is created primarily for aesthetic purposes, rather than practical ones. It is art for art's sake, as opposed to graphic design, which is art created to communicate specific ideas or concepts.

font A set of characters in typography that all share the same design characteristics.

freelancer A person who sells work or services to many different clients, rather than working for a single employer.

graduate program An educational program that provides advanced degrees, such as a master's or Ph.D., to those who have already graduated from college.

graphical user interface (GUI) A method of controlling a computer system that involves the use of icons to visually represent objects and applications, and a mouse-controlled cursor to select options from menus.

graphic design agency A business that plans and creates design projects for clients. Most will employ several graphic designers, plus support staff.

hardware The physical equipment used in a computer system.

hyperlink An element in a computer document that links to another part of the same document, or to a different document accessible over a computer network, such as the World Wide Web.

layout The way in which text and artwork are assembled on a page or screen.

logo A symbol representing a particular company or organization, designed for ready recognition.

networking The sharing of information and services among individuals and groups with a common interest.

portfolio A collection of pieces of creative work designed to display someone's skills, especially to a potential employer.

pro bono Doing work for free for altruistic purposes. It is a shortened version of the longer Latin phrase *pro bono publico*, meaning "for the common good."

software The programs and programming languages that direct the operations of a computer. It is usually divided into system software, which provides the basic operational instructions of the computer, and application software, which is used to accomplish specific tasks.

typography The style, arrangement, or appearance of the text in a document.

undergraduate program An educational program designed for undergraduates—college or university students who have yet to obtain their first degree.

user interface (UI) The means by which a person controls a software application or hardware device.

FOR MORE INFORMATION

Advertising & Design Club of Canada (ADCC)
344 Bloor Street West, Suite 205
Toronto, ON M5S 3A7
Canada
(416) 423-4113
Web site: http://www.theadcc.ca
The ADCC, a nonprofit group dedicated to encouraging excellence in Canadian advertising and design, seeks to inspire creativity, provide a forum for the exchange of ideas, and forge a sense of community and integrity among advertising and design professionals. The organization runs an annual student design competition.

AIGA, the Professional Association for Design
164 Fifth Avenue
New York, NY 10010
(212) 807-1990
Web site: http://www.aiga.org
Founded in 1914 as the American Institute of Graphic Arts, AIGA is the oldest and largest professional membership organization for design. Through AIGA, designers exchange ideas and information and advance education and ethical practice.

Design Council
Angel Building
407 St. John Street
London EC1V 4AB

United Kingdom
+44 (0) 20 7420 5200
Web site: http://www.designcouncil.org.uk
The Design Council's aim is to help people use design to transform communities, business, and the environment for the better by stimulating innovation in business and public services and inspiring new design thinking. Its Web site has a wealth of information about all aspects of design.

Graphic Artists Guild (GAG)
32 Broadway, Suite 1114
New York, NY 10004
(212) 791-3400
Web site: http://gag.org
The Graphic Artists Guild helps graphic artists (including, but not limited to, animators, cartoonists, designers, illustrators, and digital artists) build successful careers by equipping them with the skills and support they need. Resources include numerous online articles, the *Graphic Artist Guild Handbook*, and regular Webinars.

Society of Graphic Designers of Canada (GDC)
Arts Court, 2 Daly Avenue
Ottawa, ON K1N 6E2
Canada
(877) 496-4453
Web site: http://www.gdc.net
The GDC is a member-based organization of design professionals, educators, administrators, students, and associates in communications, marketing, media, and

design-related fields. It offers publications, seminars, events, conferences, and exhibits designed to build awareness of graphic design and its essential role in business and society.

Society of Illustrators, Artists and Designers (SIAD)
207 Regent Street, 3rd Floor
London W1B 3HH
United Kingdom
Web site: http://www.siad.org
The SIAD is a professional, Web-based organization that promotes excellence in all areas of visual media. It helps promote its members online and works for the protection of their intellectual property rights. Membership is open to all practicing illustrators, artists, and designers involved in any visual media.

Web Sites

Due to the changing nature of Internet links, Rosen Publishing has developed an online list of Web sites related to the subject of this book. This site is updated regularly. Please use this link to access the list:

http://www.rosenlinks.com/DCB/DDT

FOR FURTHER READING

Airey, David. *Logo Design Love: A Guide to Creating Iconic Brand Identities*. San Francisco, CA: New Riders, 2010.

Airey, David. *Work for Money, Design for Love: Answers to the Most Frequently Asked Questions About Starting and Running a Successful Design Business*. San Francisco, CA: New Riders, 2013.

Cramsie, Patrick. *The Story of Graphic Design: From the Invention of Writing to the Birth of Digital Design*. New York, NY: Abrams, 2010.

Dille, Flint, and John Zuur Platten. *The Ultimate Guide to Video Game Writing and Design*. New York, NY: Lone Eagle, 2011.

DuPuis, Steven, and John Silva. *Package Design Workbook: The Art and Science of Successful Packaging*. Reissue ed. Beverly, MA: Rockport Publishers, 2011.

Evans, Brian. *Practical 3-D Printers: The Science and Art of 3-D Printing*. New York, NY: Apress, 2012.

Hagen, Rebecca, and Kim Golombisky. *White Space Is Not Your Enemy: A Beginner's Guide to Communicating Visually Through Graphic, Web & Multimedia Design*. 2nd ed. New York, NY: Focal Press, 2013.

Hannam, Ben. *A Graphic Design Student's Guide to Freelance: Practice Makes Perfect*. Hoboken, NJ: Wiley, 2012.

Kiosoglou, Billy, and Frank Philippin. *I Used to Be a Design Student: 50 Graphic Designers Then and Now*. London, England: Laurence King, 2013.

Kleon, Austin. *Steal Like an Artist: 10 Things Nobody Told You About Being Creative*. New York, NY: Workman Publishing, 2012.

Lauer, David A., and Stephen Pentak. *Design Basics*. 8th ed. Boston, MA: Wadsworth, Cengage Learning, 2012.

McWade, John. *Before & After: How to Design Cool Stuff*. Berkeley, CA: Peachpit Press, 2010.

Peddie, Jon. *The History of Visual Magic in Computers: How Beautiful Images Are Made in CAD, 3-D, VR, and AR*. New York, NY: Springer, 2013.

Robbins, Jennifer Niederst. *Learning Web Design: A Beginner's Guide to HTML, CSS, JavaScript, and Web Graphics*. 4th ed. Cambridge, MA: O'Reilly Media, 2012.

Shaugnessy, Adrian. *How to Be a Graphic Designer Without Losing Your Soul*. New expanded ed. Princeton, NJ: Princeton Architectural Press, 2010.

Sherwin, David. *Creative Workshop: 80 Challenges to Sharpen Your Design Skills*. Cincinnati, OH: HOW Books, 2010.

Smith, Jennifer, and Jeremy Osborn. *Adobe Creative Suite 6 Design & Web Premium: Digital Classroom*. Hoboken, NJ: Wiley, 2012.

Tholenaar, Jan, Cees de Jong, and Alston W. Purvis. *Type: A Visual History of Typefaces & Graphic Styles*. Köln, Germany: Taschen, 2010.

White, Alex W. *The Elements of Graphic Design: Space, Unity, Page Architecture, and Type*. 2nd ed. New York, NY: Allworth Press, 2011.

BIBLIOGRAPHY

ADigitalDreamer.com. "How to Become a Graphic
    Designer." 2012. Retrieved April 1, 2013
    (http://www.adigitaldreamer.com/articles
    /becomeagraphicdesigner.htm).

Barnatt, Christopher. "3-D Printing." ExplainingTheFuture
    .com, March 1, 2013. Retrieved April 1, 2013
    (http://www.explainingthefuture.com
    /3-Dprinting.html).

Bentaieb, Yassine. "Interview with a Designer: Tyler
    Galpin." YassineBentaieb.com, June 20, 2011.
    Retrieved April 1, 2013 (http://www.yassinebentaieb
    .com/interviews/interview-with-a-designer
    -tyler-galpin).

Bureau of Labor Statistics, U.S. Department of Labor.
    "Graphic Designers." *Occupational Outlook
    Handbook*, March 29, 2012. Retrieved April 1, 2013
    (http://www.bls.gov/ooh/arts-and-design/graphic
    -designers.htm).

Combrinck, Tanya. "Big Question: What Skills Does a
    Digital Designer Need in 2013?" *.net*, December 10,
    2012. Retrieved April 1, 2013 (http://www
    .netmagazine.com/features/big-question-what
    -skills-does-digital-designer-need-2013).

Creativeoverflow. "24 Graphic Designers to Follow on
    Google+." July 10, 2012. Retrieved April 1, 2013
    (http://creativeoverflow.net/24-graphic-designers
    -to-follow-on-google).

Design Council. "About Design." Retrieved April 1, 2013
(http://www.designcouncil.org.uk/about-design).

Dickey, Megan Rose. "The World's 25 Best Design
Schools." BusinessInsider.com, November 23,
2012. Retrieved April 1, 2013 (http://www
.businessinsider.com/the-worlds-25-best-design
-schools-2012-11?op=1).

Graphic Design at Parkland College. "Graphic Design
History: 1985–Present: Beyond the Digital Age."
Retrieved April 1, 2013 (http://gds.parkland.edu
/gds/!lectures/history/1985/digital.html).

Koschei, Jordan. "Is Formal Design Education Necessary
for Practicing Designers?" The Industry, February
20, 2013. Retrieved April 1, 2013 (http://
theindustry.cc/2013/02/20/is-formal-design
-education-necessary-for-practicing-designers).

Lai, On Yi. "The Digital Revolution and Its Influence on
Contemporary Graphic Design." *On Air Design*,
November 5, 2011. Retrieved April 1, 2013
(http://onairdesign.wordpress.com/2011/11/05
/the-digital-revolution-and-its-influence-on
-contemporary-graphic-design).

Lee, Preston D. "10 Steps to Becoming a Successful
Freelance Designer." *Graphic Design Blender*,
February 27, 2009. Retrieved April 1, 2013
(http://www.graphicdesignblender.com/10-steps
-to-becoming-a-successful-freelance-designer).

May, Tom. "Shane Mielke: Interview." *.net*, September 5,
2007. Retrieved April 1, 2013 (http://www
.netmagazine.com/interviews/shane-mielke).

Parmenter, Sarah. "About Sarah Parmenter." Sazzy.co.uk, 2013. Retrieved April 1, 2013 (http://www.sazzy .co.uk/about).

Rutledge, Andy. "Career Path—Going Freelance." *Design Professionalism*, 2011. Retrieved April 1, 2013 (http://designprofessionalism.com/career-path -freelance.php).

Second Wednesday. "Rachel Shillcock." Retrieved April 1, 2013 (http://www.secondwednesday.org.uk /rachel-shillcock.php).

Shillcock, Rachel. "How to Get Your First Job." *.net*, January 25, 2012. Retrieved April 1, 2013 (http://www.netmagazine.com/opinions/how -get-your-first-job).

Stock-Allan, Nancy. "A Short Introduction to Graphic Design History." Retrieved April 1, 2013 (http:// www.designhistory.org).

U.S. News & World Report. "Best Graphic Design Programs—Top Graphic Design Schools." 2012. Retrieved April 1, 2013 (http://grad-schools.usnews .rankingsandreviews.com/best-graduate-schools /top-fine-arts-schools/graphic-design-rankings).

Youbee School of Design. "What Makes a Great Digital Designer?" Retrieved April 1, 2013 (http://www .yoobee.ac.nz/blog/learning-digital-designer).

INDEX

About the Author

Edward Willett is an award-winning author of more than forty books of fiction and nonfiction for children, adults, and young adults. He studied both journalism and art at college and, in addition to being a writer, designs ads, posters, billboards, programs, and Web sites for various local organizations. With his wife and daughter, Willett lives in Regina, Saskatchewan, Canada, where, in addition to writing and designing, he is a professional actor and singer. His Web sites are http://www.edwardwillett .com and http://www.wordsbywillett.com. You can also find him on Twitter (@ewillett).

Photo Credits

Cover, p. 1 smilewithme/Shutterstock.com (color palette), Igor Klimov/ Shutterstock.com (pen tablet), Umberto Shtanzman/Shutterstock.com (laptop), yienkeat/Shutterstock.com (laptop screen); p. 4 (inset) Afton Almaraz/ Photonica World/Getty Images; p. 6 Marka/SuperStock; p. 8 Apic/Hulton Archive/Getty Images; p. 10 zeber/Shutterstock.com; p. 12 (inset) yienkeat/ Shutterstock.com; p. 13 1000 Words/Shutterstock.com; p. 15 Marvi Lacar/ Getty Images; pp. 17, 29 Bloomberg/Getty Images; p. 21 © AP Images; p. 25 (inset) Ersler Dmitry/Sutterstock.com; p. 26 AntonioDiaz/Shutterstock.com; p. 33 © mark phillips/Alamy; p. 34 (inset) Hill Street Studios/Blend Images/ Getty Images; p. 35 Goodluz/Shutterstock.com; p.37 Center for Advanced Digital Applications – CADA/New York University/School of Continuing and Professional Studies; p. 38 RISD. Used with permission; p. 41 Ben Hider/ Getty Images; p. 43 (inset) mediaphotos/E+/Getty Images; p. 44 © Graphic Artists Guild; p. 49 Courtesy of AIGA, www.aiga.org. Site design: Method, Inc. (New York, NY); cover and interior pages background patterns and graphics © iStockphoto.com/Ali Mazraie Shadi, © iStockphoto.com/MISHA, © iStockphoto.com/Paul Hill, © iStockphoto.com/Charles Taylor, © iStockphoto.com/Daniel Halvorson, © iStockphoto.com/Jeffrey Sheldon; additional interior page design elements © iStockphoto.com/Lisa Thornberg (laptop pp. 4, 12, 25, 34, 43), © iStockphoto.com/abu (computer mouse).

Designer: Nelson Sá; Editor: Andrea Sclarow Paskoff;
Photo Researcher: Marty Levick